the Easter Surprise

The story of Jesus' death and resurrection from
John 20:1–20; Matthew 27:45, 54, 65; 28:2–4;
Mark 15:39, and Luke 24:3–4, 36–37 for children

Written by Claire Miller
Illustrated by Susan Spellman

CONCORDIA PUBLISHING HOUSE • SAINT LOUIS

Some surprises make you happy,
And some can make you mad.
On Easter, the world's best surprise
At first seemed really sad.

When Jesus died, the sky turned black,
The earth shook, big rocks broke.
The soldiers watching were surprised,
And then their captain spoke:

"Surely, He's the true Son of God!"
The soldiers' captain said.
Friends buried Jesus in a tomb.
The Son of God was dead!

The tomb was closed with a huge stone,
And guarded night and day
By soldiers, to keep Jesus' friends
From stealing Him away.

The soldiers had a big surprise
On Easter morning there.
An angel rolled the stone away;
He gave them quite a scare!

Then Mary, who was Jesus' friend,
Looked in the open tomb.
But Jesus was no longer there!
Her heart was filled with gloom.

"I must go tell the disciples,"
She thought, and ran away.
She didn't know the best surprise
Had happened on that day.

Mary ran to Peter and John,
With tears filling her eyes.
She said, "Our Lord Jesus is gone!"
(Another sad surprise!)

The men ran to the tomb and found
The stone was rolled away.
They saw that Jesus wasn't there,
And so they didn't stay.

Then John and Peter headed home,
But Mary turned around.
She slowly walked back to the tomb
And look at what she found . . .

She saw two angels sitting where
Jesus had been lying.
The angels saw her tears and asked
Why she had been crying.

Just then she saw a stranger there.
She wondered why He came.
She thought He was the gardener
Until He said her name.

When He said, "Mary," then she knew:
(She recognized His voice.)
Surprise! Her Jesus was alive,
And now she could rejoice!

That same day, the disciples met
Late, in the dark night.
They were surprised when Jesus stood
Among them in their sight.

"God sent Me, and I'm sending you,"
Said Jesus to the men.
"Tell everyone I died for them
And how I rose again!"

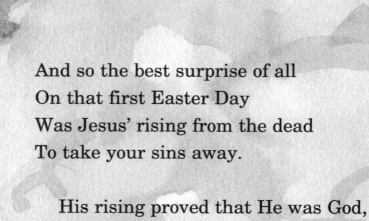

And so the best surprise of all
On that first Easter Day
Was Jesus' rising from the dead
To take your sins away.

His rising proved that He was God,
His promises are true,
And there's a place in heaven that
He's saving just for you!

Dear Parents,

   Children love surprises, and the Bible is full of them, including the amazing miracles recorded in both the Old and New Testaments. Explain to your child that the biggest and most important surprise was God's great love for His sinful people. The empty tomb on Easter was the fulfillment of His promise to send a Savior who would die for our sins and rise again to give us the hope of eternal life. It is in your child's Baptism that the story of Christ's death and resurrection becomes your child's story too.

   It is somewhat surprising that the disciples were so unprepared for the empty tomb. Jesus' death and resurrection were predicted in the Old Testament, so God had been getting the world ready for this big surprise for a long time. Jesus often reminded His followers that He had come to fulfill the prophecies. But the first reaction of His followers at the empty tomb was that someone had stolen His body. According to John 20:8–9, even Jesus' own disciples didn't understand.

   As you read this book with your child, stop to look at the pictures and discuss whether the surprises that occurred made the people happy, sad, or frightened. In the end, some of the surprises that seemed sad and scary turned out to be part of the most wonderful surprise of all time—
   the resurrection of our loving Savior.

The Author